Cast Iron

Cast Iron

by

Lisa Codrington

Playwrights Canada Press
Toronto • Canada

Playwrights Canada Press
The Canadian Drama Publisher
215 Spadina Ave. Suite 230, Toronto, Ontario CANADA M5T 2C7
416.703.0013   fax 416.408.3402
orders@playwrightscanada.com • www.playwrightscanada.com

Financial support provided by the taxpayers of Canada and Ontario through the Canada Council for the Arts and the Department of Canadian Heritage through the Book Publishing Industry Development Programme, and the Ontario Arts Council.

Front cover image "Portrait of a Grenadian Woman" by Lisa Herrera.
Cover design: JLArt
Production Editor: MZK

Library and Archives Canada Cataloguing in Publication

Codrington, Lisa
  Cast iron / Lisa Codrington.

A play.
ISBN 0-88754-842-3

  1. Barbadian Canadians--Drama. 2. Black Canadian women--Drama. 3. Immigrants--Canada--Drama. I. Title.

PS8605.O337C38 2006   C812'.6   C2006-903124-X

First edition: July 2006.
Printed and bound by Canadian Printco at Scarborough, Canada.

This play is dedicated to those that have left and to those that will come. As always this relentless pursuit of understanding is in remembrance and in anticipation of you.

Special thanks to Hughlene and Eileen Codrington for telling me stories, Elizabeth Helmers and Sheldon Rosen for supporting this play from the start, Alison Sealy-Smith and ahdri zhina mandiela for their passion and commitment and lastly Kelly Thornton for her unwavering trust in me as a writer.

I would also like to thank Nathalie Bonjour, Philip Akin, Michelle Ramsay, Alejandra Nuñez, Richard Lee, Camellia Koo, Zainab Musa, Natasha Mytnowych, Robert Gontier, Katherine Chin, Marianne McIsaac, Sophia Walker, Perry Schneiderman, Lisa Silverman, Nina Lee Aquino, Maureen LaBonte, Diane Roberts, Rhoma Spencer, Andrea Scott, Michael Miller, Brian Quirt, Angela Rebeiro, Ryerson Theatre School, Write From The Hip, Nightwood Theatre and Obsidian Theatre Company.

The world premiere of *Cast Iron* was produced by Nightwood Theatre in association with Obsidian Theatre Company at Tarragon Theatre Extra Space in 2005.

All roles   Alison Sealy-Smith

Directed by ahdri zhina mandiela
Lighting Design & Production Management by Michelle Ramsay
Set and Costume Design by Camellia Koo
Sound Design by Richard Lee and Alejandra Nuñez
Stage Management by Andrea Schurman
Assistant Lighting Designer: Aleksandra Podbereski
Apprentice Director: Christine Nicole Harris
Associate Production Management by Shauna Janssen
Production Assistant: Afrakaren Nile
Double Bass: Kieran Overs

The Playwright acknowledges the assistance of the 2004 Banff playRites Colony—a partnership between the Canada Council for the Arts, The Banff Centre for the Arts, and the Alberta Theatre Projects.

Cast Iron was publicly workshopped at Factory Theatre, Toronto, Canada, as part of the 2004 CrossCurrents Festival.

Cast Iron was developed at Nightwood Theatre as part of the Groundswell Festival.

Cast Iron was first presented by Back Row Theatre Company at the 2002 Fringe of Toronto Theatre Festival at the Robert Gill Theatre, with the following company:

All roles   Lisa Codrington

Directed by Elizabeth Helmers
Produced by Lisa Codrington and Elizabeth Helmers
Stage Managed by Katherine Chin
Dramaturged by Sheldon Rosen

Let me tell you a little story bout a brea'fruit tree,
Dat was plant by a man from across a de sea,
An feed to a monkey forced in de gullie,
Dat also was ship by de man cross de sea,
Who is boast no more teef dan one two an tree,
One more dan enough dough, tuh holla' at monkey,
Tuh "GO, AN GUH LONG, AN CLIMB UP DAT DAMN TREE,
TUH GET, ME SOME BREA'FRUIT TUH EAT WIT MY TEA!"

> Cast Iron *is comedy with a tragic ending. There is no need for big production element to make it fly, the story should be enough. The play is written in Bajan dialect.*

The Storyteller:

Libya Geraldine Atwell is the storyteller. She tells her story to the audience who she sees as an unexpected visitor, her nephew Winston-James Blackwell. NOTE: Libya never sits back as the storyteller, her stories are active confessions, and as the play progresses she becomes more of an active participant within them.

Libya Geraldine Atwell is a seventy-five-year-old woman filled with contradictions. On one hand she is a nursing home resident suffering from diabetes, but on the other hand she is a strong and determined survivor who has successfully evaded her haunting past for over forty years. Libya dresses warmly and in layers. She wears a housedress over a nightgown, longjohns, wool socks, slippers and a scarf tied around her head. Her clothes are comfortable, affordable and sensible.

The Characters:

Cast Iron is a one-woman memory play. As the storyteller, Libya takes on the voice, physicality and emotions of the characters from her past in Barbados. Libya's past completely contrasts her present. While the present is cold, sterile and stagnant the past is hot, colourful and alive. In the beginning Libya is in complete control of how and when she plays the characters from her past, but as the play continues the characters gain momentum and begin to invade and possess Libya.

NOTE: There are no blackouts or costume changes when Libya takes on the characters from her past, this transition should be done purely through voice and physicality.

Gracie Constance (nee Winston) Blackwell is Libya's half sister on her mother's side.
Gracie is physically and intellectually demanding (bossy). Her body sharply bursts indirectly and unexpectedly through space like fireworks. Gracie often waits. These waits are beats that should not be rushed over, because like the punctuation, they drive the rhythm of her speech.

Stacy Mae Winston is Libya's grandmother on her mother's side. Stacy Mae has not left her house in over thirty years. She pulses with paranoia and fear and speaks in stutters and spurts with scattered moments of calmness and clarity. Underneath everything Stacy Mae has a core of vulgarity.

Santiford Theopholis Atwell is Libya's Father.
Santiford communicates in low direct grumbles like military personnel and moves like a caged gorilla. His head is constantly down as if he's looking for something he's lost. He rarely if ever looks anyone in the eye.

James Darlington Blackwell is Gracie's love interest/husband. James is slow and smooth. His energy begins circulation in his pelvis and then ripples through the rest of his body like a wave. His speech and body flow in the same way. Basically James melts everything he comes in contact with.

Winston-James Blackwell is James and Gracie's son, Libya's nephew. He is the one Libya is speaking to.

The Red Woman is an invisible spirit that can be felt but not seen. She is the one Libya is running from.

The Family History:

Robert Charles Winston died old and fat upon his back. He was a White plantation and slave owner and Libya's great great great grandfather.

Charles Winston died old and plump and stiff as a stump after a bump. He was a White plantation owner and Libya's great great grandfather.

Mary Elizabeth Hamperton died during a full moon before her flowers had the opportunity to bloom. She ignored many a case of white lace and a Black face engulfed in her husband's embrace. She was Libya's great great grandmother and Charles Winston's White wife.

Tabetha Winston died in her middle years consumed by her fears. She was the legitimate White daughter of Charles Winston and Libya's great grandmother.

Boy Boy Brooks died in his threes while overseas after a big sneeze caused him to choke on two peas. He was a Black sugar cane cutter, Tabetha Winston's lover and Libya's great grandfather.

Stacy Mae Winston was Tabetha and Boy Boy's illegitimate and biracial daughter and Libya's grandmother. She longed for meat, and the day she did not have to retreat, and stare out the window in defeat, because there was no strength left in her feet.

Buddy was Stacy Mae's Black boy and Libya's grandfather. All that's known is that this Black man had no home because he liked to roam all alone, suck the marrow out of a nice piece of bone, and bite into sweet pieces of cassava pone without having to worry about answering the phone.

Margaret Winston was Stacy Mae and Buddy's only daughter and Libya's and Gracie's mother. Apparently she was addicted to (Epsom) salts and men that could waltz.

Santiford Theopolis Atwell was one of Margaret's ex-lovers and Libya's father. He was a betting man without a plan.

Gracie Constance (nee Winston) Blackwell was Margaret's daughter and Libya's half sister. She was a woman who inflicted strife on just about everybody's life so that she could become James Blackwell's wife.

James Darlington Blackwell was Gracie's love interest/husband. Now yuh may not be able tuh see he, but yuh know when he around, cause yuh is bound tuh feel yuhself surroun by he.

Winston-James Blackwell is Libya's nephew and the son of James and Gracie. He is a lost soul.

The Red Woman is and was a butcher of sorts. Some say she was a louse others say she was a mouse, one thing they all agree on is that they wouldn't want her in their house.

Libya Geraldine Atwell is the storyteller and the last one left. She has sprung from all of the above so is therefore a mixture of self-hate and love.

NOTE: New scenes do not indicate breaks or blackouts, they indicate shifts in time and space. The action in the present takes place in real time while the action in the past jumps around in time.

Scene 1

LIBYA's room.
Late evening.
LIBYA age 75.
LIBYA's small room at the Red River Health Centre
and Personal Care Home in the north end of Winnipeg,
Manitoba. It is a dark and windy winter evening (about
a quarter to eight). The moonlight streaming through
the small window in LIBYA's room is just enough to
illuminate her. She paces and quietly rants in protest of
the nurses, doctors, visitors, residents and intercom
pages making noise in the hallway outside her room.
Frustrated, LIBYA stares out the window. The hallway
sounds begin to fade and the clanking sound of the
heater in her room becomes audible as the wind shakes
the trees outside. The sound builds and morphs into
sugar cane swept aside by a machete. LIBYA stands
silent until she is ambushed by a sharp cutting pain in
her belly. This is the first time LIBYA has felt the call of
the Red Woman in over forty years.

LIBYA

Oh Lawrd! *(to the Red Woman)* Ha! You t'ink you gine
catch me, but you can'. Just wait… just you wait nuh. Yuh
ain' even cut muh! Dis here is a piece a gas… it gine ease
off soul. *(LIBYA rubs her belly.)* Den I gine come fuh yuh!
(The rusting in the cane disappears and the lights in LIBYA's
room snap up.)

Scene 2

LIBYA's room.
Late evening.
LIBYA age 75.

LIBYA

(out to the audience) Hallow? Hallow? What yuh want?
GET de HELL outta my room fore I lick yuh upside de
head wit muh cast iron! Who de BLAST you t'ink you is,
an what de hell kinda monkey manners yuh is use tuh

enter de place? Yuh CAN' just WALK in a person ROOM!
Yuh supposed tuh KNOCK, an den WAIT fuh dem tuh
SAY, "WHO DAT?" Doan mine if de door OPEN, nor if
de ROOF blow off, yuh must STILL say who you is fore
yuh is enter a person room… SO GET DE HELL OUT!

> *LIBYA approaches.*

Who?
Triston? Who de hell is Triston?
Youse, who?
Stan where you is!
Triston-James? I ain' know nobody name Triston-James.
Gracie?
My sister Gracie dead! How de hell you is she, she…
she—
SHE SON… From Barbados? Oh, Winston-James
Blackwell—
Yes, yes I am Libya Geraldine Atwell. I KNOW who I is.
You ole auntie mine ain' gone yet soul—

(LIBYA retreats.) Stan where yuh is! I rader you not get
suh close. Alla wunna out der always bringin de flu in
here… killin alla we. Mine you if yuh kill half a we wit
de flu, dat might open up some beds. Lawrd knows dem
always carryin on about, "not enough beds." So maybe
I will shake you han. Den dey can cover muh up… wheel
muh out… an lef me in de hallway till dey get space in de
morgue.

But later… fuh now stan where you is.

I ain' know de body was you yuh. I ain' remember de last
time I see you… it been dunkey years, but I get de face
recognize now. You got you muder big mout an you fader
Black face. Shut off de light an you disappear…. Except
fuh you big eyes.

Yuh lucky I ain' lic out you big eyes fuh blastin true my
door like so. Yuh is have tuh protect yuh self in dis place
cause yuh ain' know who gine come true de door. But
I guess dis mussy be how alla wunna is enter a room in

Barbados dese days. Glad I lef den, I ain' able wit dat
soul.

Pause. LIBYA stares at WINSTON-JAMES.

I wouldn't sit der if I was you yuh. Dat chair is dirty
boy... yuh is liable tuh get TB. Alla de people in dis
blasted place is got TB. Coughin an spreadin dey germs.
Like dis room here is need a whole bottle a bleach t'row
pun de florin tuh kill de smell a de last soul who die here.
I here t'ree mumfs now, an I still see he hair an smell he
stink all over de blasted place. De only t'ing dat is clean is
de bed, cause I is soak muh sheet wit water every night
suh as tuh get new one put on in de mornin. Blasted
housekeepin in dis place ain' ever hear of a mop an pail.
All dem do is sweep an dust. Dustin what? Do you see
any fine china in here? It a room wit a rust up ole bed, an
a hardback chair dat is pain yuh boxie baaaad mannnn...

*LIBYA stares at WINSTON-JAMES then sucks her
teeth.*

Suh what, we is gine stan up like dis de whole time you
here? Wha'yuh come here fuh? A piece a talk? You an me
ain' nuh friends. I ain' see you in over forty years, what
de hell we gine talk bout? De people here in Canada is de
same as dem back home. Alla de Black people you see
here dat get dey stay is runnin all about de place buildin
up a bundle a big house in de outskirts, workin t'ree jobs
tuh pay fuh it, an prayin in church every Sunday tuh win
de Lotto six-forty-nine. Dat ain' fuh me boy cause in de
end we is all gonna end up in de same place. *(quietly)*
A brown skin one dat usta turn she nose up at me on de
bus, WHO I KNOW had a bundle a big house, is now
lyin up in a room smaller dan dis. But even dough she
got tubes down she t'roat an life-water hook up in she
arm, she still turnin she nose up at me. Black people is de
worst people in de world soul. Gawd mek a mistake
when he mek we. But all you all back home in Barbados
is de same. Alla wunna t'ink everybody dat gone
overseas got somet'ing but we ain' got nutin'. Dat why
I never guh back home. You t'ink I want tuh listen tuh

alla wunna askin why I ain' bring dis, an why I ain'
send dat. I guess I could guh back now cause everybody
I know der dead.
My reckless fader dead...
My half n' half gra'muder dead...
My licorice muder dead...
You Black face fader dead—

> *Pause.*

You muder?
How you mean, 'what about you muder?'
Look, you muder, my sister Gracie... my half sister as de
Canadians is say, dead every sense. *We family die off fast
soul. De Lawrd ain' interested in kepin none a we around long,*
cept fuh me an I ain' interested in talkin bout she. Beside
I ain' like tuh talk ill a de dead and I ain' got nut'ing good
tuh say bout dat long-legged loud-mout Black bitch
Gracie!

> *LIBYA gets a cutting pain in her belly but hides it as
> the wind outside builds.*

Look, I sorry you come alla dis way... cause I doan have
anyt'ing good tuh say tuh you... and I ain' want tuh spen
what little life I got lef listenin tuh a big man like you run
yuh mout bout what happen tuh you over de last forty
years, nor guh on bout how yuh wish yuh had know you
muder an—

> *LIBYA gets another cutting pain in her belly but
> continues to hide it as the wind gains strength and the
> heater kicks in.*

Look, yuh too late.
I have *held my tongue* fuh so long.
I mean, where was you before? Where was you when Mr.
and Mrs. Wasserstine t'row me outta dey house an intuh
dis nursin home? I work fuh dem fuh over t'irty years.
I cook an clean fuh two generations of dey family but
dem still turn muh out... tellin me I need tuh be in here
cause a my diabetus—
Diabetus my ass! Dem done wit me, but now you callin

on me. Yuh empty an yuh come tuh Libya so she can fill yuh up. But not wit food, not in dis day an age but wit answers. But my days in domestic done. I ain' got nuh damn t'ing tuh tell you suh lef dis place! Guh long and get outta my chair cause I ain' invite you tuh sit down an I sure as shite ain' invite you tuh come alla de way from Barbados tuh Winnipeg in de middle a winter.
It too cole here tuh be playin de fool soul.

> *LIBYA gets another cutting pain that she cannot hide. The wind explodes into a rumble and the sound of sugar cane swept aside by a machete grows. LIBYA attempts to ignore the pain and talk to WINSTON-JAMES but by the end of the next short speech she can't help but speak to the Red Woman.*

Look,
Dat ain' you name pun de door…
Nor none a you t'ings in de drawer.
Dis here is my place.
Libya Atwell room t'ree-fifty-two: diabetic, mince meal, cause I got no teef tuh CHEW.
I got glaucoma dat is increase de pressure in my right an lef eye, An tugeder it gine blow me up an mek me lie down an DIE.
But fuh now I still know dat I is GOT enough SIGHT, Tuh FINE you an PELT you wit ALLA my MIGHT!

> *LIBYA is hit with a final sharp cutting pain. She rubs her belly as she warns the Red Woman.*

I gine tek my cast iron an mash up you face bad man! You may have catch everybody else but I get dis far, an yuh lie if you t'ink I gine let you catch me—
(to WINSTON-JAMES) Who? Who de hell you t'ink I talkin to? You!
Wait. Wait. Wait.
Nurse? Wha'yuh callin out for nurse fuh? LOOK, I ain' need no damn nurse tuh mek me feel better. If I ever fine myself feelin better it is because I dead soul, suh just wait.
A woman is have tuh talk tuh she pain if dat is all she got… suh wait.

Silence.

I mean, I taught you come here fuh a piece a talk.
I taught you want tuh hear story bout you muder.
Come den an sit yuh Black ass down. *(LIBYA laughs and sucks her teeth.)*
LAWRD, you is wait just like Gracie! You muder torment an exile me from de first day I meet she till de day she die. *(as GRACIE) Look, I ain' want yuh tuh play my game. Especially since you gone an uproot a piece a sugar cane you was only supposed tuh name.*

Scene 3

Inside Winston Sugar Cane Plantation.
Midday in the hot sun.
LIBYA age 8.
GRACIE age 11.
Sugar cane rustles in the wind as GRACIE exiles.
LIBYA from the cane.

GRACIE

(to LIBYA) Ain' you know we gra'ma is de gra'daughter a Charles Winston who usta own allla dis sugar cane plantation. She muder was Charles Winston White daughter, an she fader a Black cane cutter an I doan t'ink none a dem would like tuh see what you gone an do in dis here sugar cane, fuh trut. Lef de cane Libya.

LIBYA

(to WINSTON-JAMES) Gracie was raise by we gra'muder in a broken down squatter dat cross de road from Winston Sugar Cane Plantation. I was raise by my fader on Shipley Sugar Cane Plantation side. I was eight when I first meet Gracie. She was eleven and had a big soft soursop head, a loud stout smellin push up mout an long tin sugar cane legs *(LIBYA impersonates GRACIE.)* Every Saturday my fader drop me at my gra'muder house. De man need someone tuh watch over me while he bettin at de track. *(as SANTIFORD) Everyt'ing on Number 35 Black Thunder.*

Scene 4

*The road that separates Winston Sugar Cane
Plantation from LIBYA's grandmother's house.
Early morning, the sun is rising.
LIBYA age 8.
The faint sound of dogs, chickens and goats can be
heard as SANTIFORD drops LIBYA off at her
grandmother's house for the first time.*

SANTIFORD

(to LIBYA) Libya, what happen when a White plantation
owner daughter get mix up wit a poor Black cane cutter
an he "sword?" Your gra'muder, a half n' half picknee
who is run she mout worse dan a madmun. *(laugh)* You
muder was de same way suh I lef she, den Gawd tek
she... BUT DAT AIN' TUH SAY dat I ain' want yuh tuh
know you gra'muder... nor you sister... suh guh long.
You ain' see Gracie der stanin up waitin fuh you tuh
come an play?

LIBYA

(to WINSTON-JAMES) All Gracie is have tuh do is WAIT.
Like you, stanin up der waitin tuh hear bout you muder,
an all pun a sudden I talkin bout she. Gracie would wait,
an alla de chil'ren pun Winston Plantation side would
pour like grain a rice out of a bag dat brek open, cryin out
(as the children) Graaaacieeee, Naaaame some sugar
caaaane aftuh we! Stupid ass chil'ren skinnin dey teet an
stannin up stiff like dey tryin tuh avoid de lash in class.
An yuh muder der like a headmaster, givin lecture fore
she let any a we play—

Scene 5

Just outside Winston Sugar Cane Plantation.
Midday in the hot sun.
LIBYA age 8.
GRACIE age 11.
GRACIE is preparing her friends to play in the cane
field.

GRACIE
> *(to the audience)* Name Every Piece a Sugar Cane in
> Winston Plantation, *(GRACIE points to herself.)* MY
> plantation. My mummy say, "everyt'ing including sugar
> cane is need a name, or else it get tek up by de devil an
> die in shame." SO, let we go name some sugar cane...
> *(takes a breath in)* OH, but mine dis here, it a dangerous
> game runnin true Winston Plantation sugar cane. People
> is get cut up runnin true de cane... well all except dose
> dat is related by name *(GRACIE points to herself.)* Gracie
> Winston. *(GRACIE takes a breath in.)* SO, dat why alla
> wunna can only come in dis cane, if I give a piece of it
> you name, *(waits)* cause I own it. My family is de only one
> tuh avoid de RED WOMAN sword, an if yuh all follow
> me, DAT will be you reward. *(GRACIE takes in a breath.)*
> BUT, if I fine any one a yuh all suckin on de stalk or
> stealin from de crop, I will call fuh de RED WOMAN tuh
> chase you till yuh drop, an after alla wunna stop, I ain'
> afraid tuh get she tuh cut off yuh top. *(GRACIE takes in
> a breath.)* SO, Tracy an Clotell Morgan next tuh you...
> muh little sistuh Lib-ya hidin behine you... an ohhh
> yesss, my BIG BLACK BOY *(waits)* yes James dat is you!
> Alla you please come run behine me, an hole tight a de
> cane I give yuh tuh name. *(GRACIE takes in a breath.)* OH,
> but watch fuh de RED WOMAN dat stomp true dis cane,
> an shout out, "IT GONNA RAIN" if she catch sight a we
> game. Alla wunna come we is gonna mek some fun!

LIBYA
> *(to WINSTON-JAMES)* Fun what? You muder pullin me
> by de arm MEKIN me run true Winston Sugar Cane
> Plantation fearin fuh de Red Woman? You mussy hear

bout de Red Woman growin up on Winston Plantation side… especially after wha'happen tuh you muder.

Scene 6

Inside Winston Sugar Cane Plantation.
Midday in the shaded cane field.
LIBYA age 8.
GRACIE age 11.
GRACIE explains the myth of the Red Woman as she leads LIBYA and her friends deep into the cane field.

GRACIE
(to LIBYA and the audience)
Old Charles Winston who first own dis cane,
Get he meat from de butcher who live down de lane.
But dis one time…
De butcher ha fine…
Dat she ain' have nuh meat fuh Charles Winston tuh eat.
So she kill some loud mout chil'ren in de cane,
An wrap dem up like meat, (as if dey de same).
But when she business get back pun it feet,
An she bring Charles Winston, sweet pig meat tuh eat,
He say, "Grrrahhh! Dis ain' as sweet as de meat I get las week!"
So she run true de cane an start cuttin again.
An when she han start tuh turn red,

> *GRACIE looks down at her hands and then shows them to LIBYA.*

An alla de people children end up dead,
People change an call she de RED WOMAN instead.
De ole people is say she die…
But we gra'ma say, "it is ah bundle ah lie,"
So if yuh hear de RED WOMAN t'rashin true de cane—
Whooosh wooosh woosh!
Stop where yuh is an shout out, "IT GONNA RAIN!"

LIBYA

> *(to WINSTON-JAMES)* Gracie's game lead me right down de paf tuh de Red Woman.

GRACIE

> *(to LIBYA)* Libya you will go... oh no I am goin dat way... oh an dat way is fuh Tracy an Clotell. NO, not dat way girl, dat way fuh my boy James. Libya you will go... dis way.
>
> *GRACIE points down an ominous looking path that leads deeper into the sugar cane.*

LIBYA

> *(to WINSTON-JAMES)* She mek me she own sister, run de way wit de most spread out... swibble up... trample up, hungry lookin piece a sugar cane growin.

GRACIE

> *(to LIBYA)* GO!

LIBYA

> *(LIBYA moves down the path looking for an adequate piece of cane to name. Suddenly she feels the presence of the Red Woman and she mouths, then whispers "it gonna rain.")* It gonna rain. It gonna rain. *(LIBYA is hit with a quick cutting pain in her belly, like the jab of a sword. Unscathed she begins to yell out, "it gonna rain.")* It gonna rain! IT GONNA RAIN! *(to WINSTON-JAMES)* I ain' even have tuh turn round tuh know it was de Red Woman. I just tek up de firs hungry piece a cane I see an run strait back de way I came. IT GONNA RAIN, IT GONNA RAIN! My eye catch Gracie and I grabble she up too. IT GONNA RAIN, IT GONNA RAIN!

Scene 7

Outside Winston Sugar Cane Plantation.
Midday, in the hot sun.
LIBYA age 8.
GRACIE age 11.
GRACIE lectures LIBYA in front of her friends.

GRACIE

(to LIBYA) Lib-ya, *(GRACIE waits.)* why yuh gone an shout out, "it gonna rain?"
I ain' see nuh RED WOMAN in dis here cane.

GRACIE takes a breath in, then waits a moment.

Look, I ain' want yuh tuh play my game.
Especially since you gone leffin me mash up an maim,
Cause you t'rashin true de cane,
Uprootin a piece you was only supposed tuh name,
While all de resta we tryin tuh play my game.
Lef de cane Lib-ya cause YOU is de only RED WOMAN here.

Shouting and taunting LIBYA.

RED WOMAN, RED WOMAN, WRAP YUH DAMN MEAT,
WIT YUH BLOOD RED HANDS, AN YUH BUTCHERIN SHEET!
RED WOMAN, RED WOMAN, WANNA TEK WE LIFE,
WIT YUH BLOOD RED HANDS, AN YUH BUTCHERIN KNIFE!

LIBYA

(to WINSTON-JAMES) Gracie an she friends shout suh hard I ain' get a chance tuh tell she dat, DE RED WOMAN WILL CUT OFF YOU PIG EARS... AN RIP OUT YOU LOUD MOUT... TEAR OFF YOU BLACK FACE AN CUFF YUH IN YOU BIG TEEF! Too bad cause she do. Gracie ain' believe me an hear yuh shout, she get cut up by de Red Woman.
Dat is it... end of story.

The sounds of the nursing home begin to fade back in.

Yuh can stop waitin now. I have t'ings tuh do. *(pause)* Just cause I in a nursin home doan mean dat I ain' have t'ings tuh do. *(LIBYA begins to do leg exercises.)* De doctor always t'reatnin tuh cut off my legs if dem is get cole an stiff, so I is have tuh kep de blood circulatin. I am de last diabetic in dis place still able tuh walk soul. Alla de rest a dese stupid ass people in here let gan'green eat up dey foot. But I ain' like dese White people soul, I can' afford tuh go an buy false foot, an I ain' want tuh be tie up in nuh wheelchair. Beside who gine push me bout? You an you big eyes? No tanks! I barely convince de nurse tuh let me do exercise in my room. She rader me walk wit she up an down dat blasted hallway. But I am already on my way tuh deaf an ain' need tuh race de rest a de dyin tuh be de first tuh my grave. Stupid ass nurses tryin tuh mek it like a game sayin, de first tuh be done gettin a prize. Fuget dat boy, I have diabetus an de las t'ing I want is tuh fine out de prize a bundle a tubes tie round my mout, shove up my ass an squeeze out my nose. I ain' want tuh get catch like you muder suh I have tuh kep fit, cause, DE RED WOMAN WILL CUT OFF YOU PIG EARS... AN RIP OUT YOU LOUD MOUT... TEAR OFF YOU BLACK FACE AN CUFF YUH IN YOU BIG TEEF! *(LIBYA gets hit with a cutting pain in her belly that transforms into two hard lashes from her father.)* AYE! AYE!

Scene 8

*The road that separates Winston Sugar Cane
Plantation from LIBYA's grandmother's house.
Late evening.
LIBYA age 8.*

SANTIFORD
(spanking LIBYA) What de hell you cryin out fuh de Red Woman fuh? She dead... but de way you carryin on she might wake from she grave.

Look Libya, de Red Woman ain' cut off no one pig ears,
nor no one loud mout. Dat is a bundle a foolishness. She
was a butcher, an dat was it. Dem call she de Red Woman
cause she ain' never tek time tuh wash she hans after she
handle de meat so dem turn red. Dat why she die off suh
fast. She get tome. Doan mine Gracie an she friends. You
gra'muder is de one who fill Gracie head wit a whole
lotta shite bout de Red Woman. You gra'muder ain' ever
lef dat house fuh fear a de Red Woman. She mek
Margaret de same way, dat why she die out suh fast. Suh
as soon as you pass true Margaret t'ick t'ighs I tek you de
hell outta dat blasted house. I barely miss gettin hit uptop
de head wif de cast iron, you gra'muder cryin out like
a madmun, "RED WOMAN, RED WOMAN!" But yuh
ole enough tuh close yuh ears tuh alla dat shite now, suh
stay inside wit you gra'muder. Lef de cane Libya, cause if
you run true de White man cane, you gine get cut wit he
sword cause dem pun Winston is lef dey sword in de
cane fuh any madmun tuh pick up an cut little girl tail
up. Lef de cane Libya.

LIBYA

(to WINSTON-JAMES) I have been fightin off de Red
Woman since I was eight years ole cause my fader can'
kep away from de race track pun a Saturday.
(as SANTIFORD) Everyt'ing on number twenty-two Tropical
Transit! Lefin me at my gra'muder was wort de risk.

Scene 9

Outside LIBYA's grandmother's house.
Morning.
GRACIE age 11.

GRACIE

(to LIBYA) Pst… pst… if yuh goin inside wit gra'ma stay
close tuh de window, so dat if she hand get hot, yuh can
just jump out. (GRACIE takes in a breath.) Ohhhhh, an
doan let she tek yuh back intuh de kitchen. I hear we usta
have a NEXT sister, an one day gra'ma mistake she fuh

de Red Woman, hit she upside de head wit de cast iron
den t'row she in de stone oven.

GRACIE demonstrates as she chants.

RED WOMAN, RED WOMAN, WRAP YUH DAMN
MEAT
WIT YOU BLOOD RED HANDS, AN YOU BUTCHERIN
SHEET...

LIBYA

(to WINSTON-JAMES, as she gets a cutting pain in her belly)
Visitin hours is six-t'irty tuh eight-t'irty an it almost half
past. I have exercises tuh do, and I CAN' do dem wit you
big eyes lookin back at me suh guh long. Get de hell outta
my room! What yuh come here fuh? You is who bring
me alla dis pain. Askin alla you questions. *(mimicking
WINSTON-JAMES)* Tell me bout my muder, tell me how
she die...
I was fine...

LIBYA mumbles to herself.

My belly all fill up wit gas. It is get vex wit me when
I doan eat at a proper time. I have diabetus... an de las
t'ing I want is tuh fall down a bad fees an bruise up my
foot cause instead a eatin I tellin story. I ain' nuh spring
chicken, I is have tuh eat.
(to WINSTON-JAMES) I ain' like de food dem is serve
here. It ain' got nuh taste. If I still had my gra'muder cast
iron I could mek up salt fish an cou cou... peas an rice an
stew beef...

I ain' know how an when my gra'muder get she cast iron,
but by de time she give it tuh me it already look like it
been around fuh dunkey years. When I firs meet my
gra'muder, she have de cast iron grip in ONE hand, an
she der hidin behine it, tremblin fuh fear a de Red
Woman.

Scene 10

Inside LIBYA's grandmother's house.
Midday.
LIBYA age 8.

STACY MAE

(to LIBYA, STACY MAE is holding onto the cast iron with one hand and pointing out the window with the other) Oh, my, my, my… look, look, look! Yuh see she? She in a broad rim hat… an, an wearin a flower print top… tuck intuh a green a-line skirt. She starin strait back at we.
(whispering) Yuh see she red hands an sharp cleaver knife. Ohhh, Libya I know she want tuh come intuh dis house an tek my life. The Red Woman was tuh kill me while I was still inside my muder, but I escape she knife an she never fugive me fuh dat. She, she was usta comin in here… just tekin up what she want.
But those days gone.

STACY MAE holds out the cast iron.

Come my girl… tek muh cast iron, cause no man can stan pun he two feet after yuh hit he upside de head wit it!

STACY MAE gives the cast iron to LIBYA.

LIBYA

(to WINSTON-JAMES, taking the cast iron from STACY MAE) It like it weigh more dan me soul. It was big an black, an I bet if you want you could fry an serve me up in dat monkey pot. I get suh used tuh holin on tuh it I could lift it wit one arm. *(LIBYA demonstrates with two swings as she shouts.)* BAM BAM!

STACY MAE

(to LIBYA) In de ole days dis house usta be a slave quarters. It where de master, Robert C. Winston come an pick out what slave he want fuh what. I was tuh call he Great Gran'fader *(STACY MAE makes the sign of the cross.)* (Gawd rest he soul). I ain' never meet he. I ain' even know de man I was tuh call Gran'fader… Charles Winston, *(STACY MAE makes the sign of the cross.)*

(Gawd rest he soul too). He ain' ever use dis place as slave quarters… but what he do wit it is practically de same t'ing. *(STACY MAE begins to giggle.)* It, it w-where he tek he little Black girls. Well, well actually dey tek him in de cane field an *(STACY MAE thrust her pelvis forward twice as she shouts:)* BAM BAM *(STACY MAE holds her hands out in front of her belly.)* when dey belly get big and swell up… he bring dem tuh dis house tuh get de chile cut out. An de Red Woman is who do it. She do it on she way tuh deliver meat. Comin intuh dis house playin butcher wit one package a meat in she right han, an a empty sheet in she left. But, but look girl… when she lef she have two package a meat. Dis de truf… my muder tell me. When my muder was a little girl she see de Red Woman berryin de package wit de baby in de cane, an deliverin de package wit de meat tuh my Gran'fader. But one time de Red Woman get de packages mix up, *(STACY MAE giggles.)* an BAM BAM Charles Winston *(STACY MAE makes the sign of the cross.)* (Gawd rest he soul) get a meat he ain' expect. Dat how my muder know dat when she fader tell she tuh come tuh dis house, it cause he had find out she pregnant by a Black cane cutter. Suh she lock de door tight an kep me safe. I do de same wif Margaret… *(STACY MAE makes the sign of the cross.)* (Gawd rest she soul) but Margaret let Gracie run wild, an let you fader tek you away. But now you back *(STACY MAE raises her arms and looks to the sky.)* (tank de lawrd) an you gine kep me safe cause you gine stay inside wif gra'ma.

LIBYA

(to WINSTON-JAMES) My gra'muder could go on like dat all day. She ain' never like tuh see me let go a dat cast iron. Fullin up she guts wit food was de only t'ing dat calm she down… cause it involve me holdin on tuh de cast iron. She would stare out de window at de brea'fruit tree an shout out, *(as STACY MAE)* uhh… uhh hambone, sweet potato, dumpin an fresh thyme. I jus t'row dem all in de pot an it mek food. Over de next few years I get lock up in my gra'muder house every Saturday mekin bakes… but it alright. De more I fill she guts de calmer

she get. I know Gracie feel dis too cause she start peepin true de window in at we. Gracie interest lef de cane and she start stayin inside. BUT, sayin it temporary, playin a new game called—

Scene 11

Outside LIBYA's grandmother's house.
LIBYA age 11.
GRACIE age 14.

GRACIE   *(to LIBYA)*
My daddy live in Canada an he is gonna send fuh muh.
He is have inside toilet, runnin water and lectricity nuh.
Everybody der is rich, cause de streets is pave of gold,
An nobody ever die, cause der is no such t'ing as old,
Firs time he der, he t'ink he see snow fallin from de sky,
But it just a bundle a White people, wit dey chest held high.

LIBYA

(to WINSTON-JAMES) Every Saturday I come an fine she mekin up nut'ing but rhymes while my gra'muder starve out an cryin fuh a piece a food. An Gracie ain' doin a damn t'ing tuh help she. Even if I cook all day Saturday I still ain' able tuh mek enough food tuh calm she fuh de week, suh I start comin more often, till I fine dat I ain' ever lefin.

Scene 12

Outside LIBYA's grandmother's house.
Saturday night.
LIBYA age 11.

SANTIFORD

(to LIBYA) Gawd Blain, we is all gonna lef... you is gonna lef... I is gonna lef... alla we is gine lef. I sooner dan de rest cause I ain' got nobody tuh cook my blasted food.

Suh come, come let we lef dis place. I ain' want you livin wit dat madmun.

LIBYA

(to WINSTON-JAMES) My gra'muder was goin down an needed someone tuh tek care a she, suh I close de door an watch my fader leave tuh bet all he have left on *(as SANTIFORD) Number 17 Colonial Cornucopia!* Soon as Gracie see I ain' leffin, it turn intuh anoder game fuh she—

Scene 13

Inside LIBYA's grandmother's house.
LIBYA 14.
GRACIE 17.
GRACIE is feeding STACY MAE.

GRACIE

(to LIBYA as she feeds STACY MAE) Lib-ya *(waits)* Lib-ya *(waits)* Lib-ya.
I t'row yuh cast iron in de gully fuh some licorice monkey cause alla de bakes dat yuh fry up is what mek gra'ma swell up! Yuh does mek too much.
Dat why gran'ma sugar so high,
An she blind in she eye.
Always knocking t'ing bout de place,
Sayin, "I ain' got no space."
I can lower she sugar, by feedin she right,
And kepin she far way from alla you shite.
De doctor tell me dat she can only tek brof. Alla dat shite you cookin she up in de cast iron is fit fuh de trof.

LIBYA

(to WINSTON-JAMES) Gracie smart soul, over de next few years she tek up my place side a my gra'muder feedin she consommé brof like it soup tic wit ham bone an cassava. Cause she tek my cast iron, all I could do is sit in de house an LISTEN tuh my gra'muder cry out.

Scene 14

Inside LIBYA's grandmother's house.
LIBYA 20.
GRACIE 23.
A rustling of wind and cane can be heard.

STACY MAE

(to LIBYA on her deathbed) Look look look my girl, come watch de boys climb de brea'fruit tree.
Lucky it have roots tuh stay stan up while dem boys play, "I am climbin tuh de top." *(STACY MAE sucks her teeth.)*
I hope dey get t'row from de damn top!
Dey jump up an climb down as dey please,
Dey swing and break de branches as dey please.
Dey mash up de bark wit a stick,
Slash in dey name wif a knife,
Tear out de leave wif dey hans,
An den lef an go, when dey fine a green an sticky brea'fruit.
Lef de tree as if a hurricane hit it!
I wish I learn tuh climb de brea'fruit tree…
But when I was a girl I was more interested in climbin de boys dan de tree… an now I hungry… cause I ain' got no brea'fruit.
LIBYA MY GIRL! Oh, my my my my. I would love a piece a brea'fruit… oh an some cassava mash up in some soup cause muh mout is waterin' fur some soup soul… some BONE, some HAM BONE! Oh Gawd Libya I can' tek de brof no more!
(STACY MAE sees the Red Woman.) Oh lawrd… yuh see dat? Yuh see she comin? Oh my my my de Red Woman comin! LIBYA lef de soup, where de cast iron? Yuh let go a de cast iron girl? Yuh is supposed tuh be lookin out ready tuh strike she fast so. BAM, BAM! Who tell you tuh let go, WHO DE HELL TELL YOU TUH LET GO A DE CAST IRON MY GIRL? Ain' you know she always come back my girl? *(pause)* Fine den, lef dis place. Lef dis place if you gine let she catch me, JUST GET DE HELL OUT AN LEF ME WIT GRACIE!

LIBYA

> *(to WINSTON-JAMES)* I was gine tell she, *(to STACY MAE)* I will fight de Red Woman wit my bare hands an if she come in dis place I will cut she up first. AIN' NO RED WOMAN COMIN IN HERE TUH CUT OFF WE PIG EARS AN— *(Silence as LIBYA watches STACY MAE take her last breath and die.)* But before I could say anyt'ing… my gra'muder get catch—
>
> > *LIBYA gets hit with a sharp cutting pain in her belly.*

GRACIE

> *(to LIBYA)* Oh Gawd! Oh Lord! She gone Libya. De Lawrd tek she up an gone. Oh, look she eyes roll up in she head. She body gettin stif! OH LAWRD, OH GAWD, tek me instead, lef muh gra'ma! *(waits)* OH, NO wait, kep she!

Scene 15

> *LIBYA's room.*
> *Present.*
> *LIBYA 75.*
> *The wind howls.*

LIBYA

> *(to the Red Woman, as LIBYA gets hit with a sharp cutting pain in her belly)* You back den? My gra'muder ain' lie in trut! Yuh always come back even if yuh is have tuh come alla de way tuh Canada tuh kill an ole woman who already on she way tuh deaf. Hell, I ain' do a damn t'ing tuh deserve dis! *(to WINSTON-JAMES)* Gracie deserve dis! You muder is de one who let my gra'muder die! She know dat my gra'muder would fuget me soon as de taste a my bakes lef she mout so she tek way my cast iron an den tek up my place side a my gra'muder starvin she out. You is, just like you muder, tryin tuh starve muh out, empty muh so dat yuh can grab up my t'ings an guh long. Grab up t'ings yuh ain' even know yuh want. I would still be in Barbados if it ain' fuh she tekin my gra'muder house out from un'neat me. Wait. Where you goin?

Come back here. Sit you Gawd Blain ass down. I taught
you wanted tuh hear bout you muder? Lef, an you gine
do de same t'ing Gracie do tuh my gra'muder. Lef me
open tuh get catch. You can' bring alla dis up den lef me
like so jus cause yuh ain' like what yuh hear. You t'ink I is
like what I is have tuh tell?
(LIBYA sucks her teeth.) Fine den... guh long.
I last dis long fuh a reason. I ain' like de rest a dem. I ain'
gine get catch by de Red Woman. I ain' need muh cast
iron, anyt'ing will do...
(LIBYA demonstrates.) Some hot water tuh pelt in she face,
Some pencil tuh juck in she guts,
Some book tuh hit she upside she head...
(LIBYA takes two large swings.) BAM BAM!

Scene 16

The backyard of LIBYA's grandmother's house.
LIBYA age 20.
GRACIE age 23.

JAMES

*(to LIBYA with his hands up as he jumps out of the way of her
swing)* Libs it me James. I just come tuh give my
respects... suh yuh can put de cast iron down. I sorry tuh
hear you gra'muder die. But you gine be alright girl! You
gine get true. Alright? Alright. Now where is my sweet
Grace? I bring she somet'ing tuh ease de pain. *(JAMES
smiles.)*

LIBYA

(to WINSTON-JAMES) After my gra'muder dead I fine
she cast iron tuh de back a de house an nearly mistake
you fader fuh de Red Woman... you know you is look an
dress just like you fader. He lookin smart, and as Black as
night in a white button-up shirt wit de collar high, de
sleeves roll up an de front open up tuh he navel. Every
single night up until my gra'muder wake I had tuh listen
tuh James ease Gracie pain. *(as GRACIE)* Ohhhhh Jaaaames!
De man proud boy, leffin dis house skinnin he teet askin
me if he could, sooth my pain. *(to WINSTON-JAMES)*

I just tek up de cast iron an tell he strait, *I ain' got no pain*
fuh you tuh sooth, AN de pain I got, I would like tuh kep an
use at my gra'muder wake.

GRACIE

    (to LIBYA) Yuh fine yuh cast iron den? Das alright we's
    gine need food at de wake. But doan go an mek none
    a you slave bakes. Dis here is an event fuh hot tea an
    cakes.

LIBYA

    (to WINSTON-JAMES) I wouldn't call what we do fuh we
    poor great half an half gra'muder wake. Black people in
    dem days ain' have wake. De only people der is Gracie
    friends, an it ain' tek dem long tuh put on de calypso an
    start tuh jump up.

Scene 17

    Inside LIBYA's grandmother's house.
    LIBYA age 20.
    GRACIE age 23.
    Calypso music is playing at the wake.

GRACIE

    (GRACIE dances and sings a song she made up over the music
    that is playing at the wake.)
    Let me tell you a little story bout a brea'fruit tree,
    Dat was plant by a man from across a de sea,
    An feed to a monkey forced in de gullie,
    Dat also was ship by de man cross de sea,
    Who is boast no more teef dan one two an tree,
    One more dan enough dough, tuh holla' at monkey,
    Tuh "GO, AN GUH LONG, AN CLIMB UP DAT DAMN
    TREE,
    TUH GET, ME SOME BREA'FRUIT TUH EAT WIT MY
    TEA!"

LIBYA

    (to WINSTON-JAMES as she makes bakes) I spen de whole
    wake mekin food in de kitchen so dat Gracie an she
    friends have de stengfth tuh wine up un'neat each uder,

an jump up top my gra'muder grave till four day mornin.
I cook up stew food, peas an rice, black puddin an souse,
as well as my *(as JAMES) bakes*. You fader especially like
my *(as JAMES) bakes*. He almost spend de entire wake wit
me in de kitchen eatin dem strait outta de cast iron.

JAMES

(to LIBYA while eating bakes) Oooh Libya Geraldine Atwell,
these is de finest bakes I ever taste! *(quietly)* Lord, if yuh
can mek bakes like dis I wonder how yuh ca knead sweet
bread. Girl, I ain' know yuh have time tuh become a chef
always up in dis house. Oooh girl, I advise you tuh tek
yuh self up an guh long tuh France. But firs, how bout
some more a you bakes Miss Atwell?

LIBYA

(to WINSTON-JAMES) I ain' say a word, I just mek he
more... an when I finish, we eat till we guts full an we
can' even stan up. We just look at each uder greeze up
face... an swell up belly, an laugh— *(Silence as LIBYA
stares at JAMES, LIBYA as GRACIE.) James! James!* Gracie
ain' like tuh know James is interested in anyt'ing dat ain'
name Gracie.

GRACIE

(to all of the guests at the wake) James lower down dat
music. *(GRACIE waits, the music gets soft.)* Dat is good.
Okay. Tanks. *(GRACIE waits.)* Everybody I have an
announcement to make, I Gracie Winston, is havin James
Blackwell baby an we is gonna call it Winston after my
Winston Plantation... my gra'ma woulda wanted dat...
Gawd rest she soul! *(GRACIE cries out.)* Oh Lawrd... oh
Gawd... muh gra'ma dead! Why yuh tek she Lawrd? Firs
yuh tek my mummy now muh gra'ma, why man why—

LIBYA

(to WINSTON-JAMES) James ain' come back fuh no bakes
after dat suh I wash up de cast iron. I just open de pipe
more an more suh as tuh drown out she loud mout. But
I can' close my ears tuh she suh I dry off de cast iron wit
a clof tuh get it grip an I walk toward Gracie.

GRACIE

(to her guests at the wake) We ain' care if it a boy or a girl it gine be name Winston. How you mean, Winston is a nice name fuh a girl... we could call she Winnie. Ain' dat right baby? James! James... what did I just say? *(GRACIE waits.)* Dat ain what I say! No I ain' say dat! Oh lawrd, I hope you hard ears ain' get pass down tuh my Winnie—

> LIBYA throws the cast iron at GRACIE.

LIBYA

(to WINSTON-JAMES) I t'row dat cast iron at Gracie strait soul. But I miss she, an it guh long true de window. My gra'muder beautiful window. Glass all over de place.

GRACIE

(to her guests at the wake) De devil is in dat girl. I know she was in tuh Obeah, yuh know! Call back Pastor Morgan, she need a reverend!
She want tuh be de RED WOMAN wit twenty-five knife.
Cut we all up an den tek way we life.
Come James an pass me two a dem sticks,
Cause I ain' gine mis dis chance tuh give she some licks!

LIBYA

(to WINSTON-JAMES) I ain' pay she nuh mine. I jus guh long outside lookin tuh tek up my cast iron an try my luck again soul, but James beat me to it an hole Gracie back.

GRACIE

(GRACIE stands in the doorway holding onto the cast iron as she speaks to LIBYA.) I ain' want you in my house Libya. Guh long, before I tek dis t'ing and hit yuh upside de head! Yuh know I able tuh cut tail an lef yuh fuh dead! Yuh jus jealous dat my belly gine get big an full up wit life, while you own stay flat, all turn up wit strife. But dat ain' nuh fault ah mine. You is de one who decide tuh follow de RED WOMAN knife! So in turn you ain' ENTITLE TUH A LIFE! Lef my house Lib-ya. *(GRACIE slams the door in LIBYA's face.)*

LIBYA

(to WINSTON-JAMES) If she ain' slam de door in my
blasted face I woulda tell she strait, "DE RED WOMAN
WILL CUT OFF YOU PIG EARS... AN RIP OUT YOU
LOUD MOUT... TEAR OFF YOU BLACK FACE AN
CUFF YUH IN YOU BIG TEEF!"

Scene 18

In front of LIBYA's grandmother's house.
At the wake.
LIBYA age 20.

JAMES

*(JAMES hides the cast iron behind his back and speaks to
LIBYA.)* Pst! Pst... Libs. I bring you dis. *(JAMES holds out
the cast iron.)* I bring you back dis. *(JAMES offers LIBYA the
cast iron then pulls it out of reach.)* Ooooh girl... you brek
up dat window bad. Mussey be alla dem bakes you is fry
up dat mek you arms so strong. *(JAMES re-enacts LIBYA
throwing the cast iron through the window.)* Eeeeeeee
Yahhhhhhhhh! *(JAMES laughs.)* Come, come back in girl.
Gracie ain' mean tuh t'row you out. Come inside an let
we eat bakes till we guts full up. I ain' able tuh fuget you
bakes girl. Gracie can' cook like you. Here come an tek
you cast iron. *(JAMES offers the cast iron to LIBYA again
then pulls it out of reach for a second time and instead offers
her his embrace.)* Come girl... come...

LIBYA

(to WINSTON-JAMES) You fader come up behine me an
slip he arms around me *(LIBYA closes her eyes, silence, she
gets a cutting pain in her belly.)* an put my cast iron back
intuh my hand.
I tek he han from around my waist, give he back my cast
iron an I lef... I just lef James stanin der holin on tuh my
cast iron lookin stiffer dan my gra'muder in she grave.
I lef, an walk back tuh my fader house fuh de first time in
years. *(LIBYA walks to her father's house.)*

Scene 19

LIBYA's father's house.
LIBYA age 20.
NOTE: From this scene onward LIBYA's pain becomes increasingly constant.

SANTIFORD

(to LIBYA) Gawd blain, alla wunna wake finish fast.
A wake dat finish so fast ain' no use. I guess you
gra'muder t'ink because she is half-White she deserve
wake. It end up dough dat because she is half-White,
she only get half de wake.

SANTIFORD pauses as he looks LIBYA over.

I almost tek you fuh you muder when you walk true de
door.

SANTIFORD pauses as he looks LIBYA over again.

Gawd Blain, yuh-yuh is look just like she, but you is look
like a piece a pork hole up on some meat hook.
Eeeeveryyybody want tuh buy meat... but nooobody
want tuh buy you.
Yuh-yuh is still a girl, an yuh already get spoil up. At dis
age you should be a sweet piece o'pork.
But yuh is already look like—like a headless knock-
kneeded chicken runnin bout de place wit a belly full
a gas...
Dat you will soon fine,
Only get ease wit a bucket a salty brine,
An hot tea an lime... an anyt'ing else yuh can buy fuh
a dime.

Pause.

Maybe der is a Red Woman in trut... cause it look like she
tek de life outta you. I ain' suprise, alla you muder family
die out fas soul. Look tuh me like Gawd ain' interested in
kepin none a you around long. Black an White doan mix.

Pause.

Alright den, I gine tuh de track. *(He begins to leave.)*
Everyt'ing on number forty-four White Lightning!

LIBYA

(to WINSTON-JAMES) After a few mumfs my fader get
tired a lookin at me an decide he ain' comin back. An
de few pennies dat he lef in de house soon run out, so
in a few mumfs I had nuh choice but tuh go back tuh my
gra'muder house.
I ain' have no place else tuh go.
When Gracie opened up de door de first t'ing I see was
she belly all swell up big. I had fuget she was havin
a baby. Yuh'd only know if yuh look at she hard dough
cause she got she self all cover up an she ain' interested
in runnin she mout bout it nuh more. Mine you she still
interested in orderin me tuh do dis an tuh do dat.

Scene 20

*LIBYA's grandmother's house on Winston Sugar Cane
Plantation side.*
LIBYA age 20.
GRACIE age 23.
Months after the wake.
*LIBYA stands in the doorway of her grandmother's
house. GRACIE stands inside. She has just taken salts
in an attempt to stop the cutting in her belly (abort her
baby). Throughout this scene to the end of the play
GRACIE's pain increases as her abortion advances, but
she fights to stay composed throughout.*
*NOTE: From this point until the end of the play and
there is less of a clear divide between LIBYA's memories
and the present. The divide between LIBYA's pain and
GRACIE's pain also begins to blur.*

GRACIE

(to LIBYA) Look, as long as yuh kep de cast iron pun de
range we is gine get along fine. *(waits)* I have ha time tuh
fugive yuh fuh tryin tuh pelt me upside de head wit we
gra'ma cast iron. Forgiveness is de way of de lawrd soul.
(waits) Beside, I glad yuh come, I need some more Epson

Salts real fast. Yuh t'ink yuh can run tuh Mr. Buyer shop?
My belly cuttin muh bad an I just run out—
JAMES woooould go but…

LIBYA

> *(to WINSTON-JAMES)* Salts ain' do nufin but numb de
> pain an cloud you head. A little cuttin in you belly is let
> you know you is alive. Dat is why I ain' tek none a de
> tablets dem is give me here. Alla dese people in dis
> nursin home is tellin me I need tablet fuh dis an tablet fuh
> dat. I ain' want nuh tablet tuh mek my head spin like
> Gracie own. She need food not salts. I tell she strait, You
> need food. An den I put my cast iron back on de range.

> *LIBYA begins to cook.*

An hear yuh shout I start fryin up bakes, plantain, ham
an fish cakes an before yuh know it I grating my knuckle
along wit de coconut fuh sweet bread.

GRACIE

> *(to LIBYA)* When dat done mix up, how long yuh have
> tuh knead dat fuh? *(GRACIE waits.)*
> FIVE MINUTES tuh KNEAD bread!
> Well start kneadin it now den.

> *Wait.*

LOOK, lef de dough Libya… I really need yuh tuh get me
some more salts. I ain' need tuh fill my belly wit alla dis
shite—

LIBYA

> *(to GRACIE as LIBYA prepares the sweet bread)* De only way
> tuh close she mout is tuh put she tuh work. I tell she
> strait, WE MEKIN sweet bread, suh SIVE in de flour… salt…
> bakin soda an bakin powder… NOW de coconut… an now
> MIX IT ALL UP.

> *LIBYA prepares to knead the bread.*

> *AN NOW let we dirty up de place an knead de life outta dis
> dough—*

GRACIE

> *(to LIBYA)* Libya my belly is cuttin… just like we mummy. I need more salts girl. I only tek like, two… well t'ree, no wait like—like half or half cup fuh de day, fuh—fuh de week. An—an I spill de bulk of it pun de grown. No mine, I need more, Libya.

LIBYA

> *(to WINSTON-JAMES. LIBYA kneads the bread. It gets harder and harder to knead.)*
> A teaspoon a salts is clean yuh out but de amounc yuh muder had already tek would mek any man spen all day in de outhouse an all night pun de topsey.
> I tell she strait, *Yuh had enough den, salts ain' nuh good fuh yuh baby. You need food.* But she want tuh be clean out boy.

GRACIE

> *(to LIBYA quietly)* We mummy get dis too, I know you ain' know she but I watch de belly cut she so bad… it cut de life right out from she.
> I was eleven.
> It before you start comin here.
> One mornin mummy had hollar hard fuh me tuh go tuh Mr. Buyer shop an get she salts. But like you I ain' pay she nuh mine instead I guh long tuh my Winston Sugar Cane Plantation an run till de sound a de cane drown out she loud mout. At first de cane feel nice slidin cross my belly but de more I run, de more I feel like it cuttin intuh my belly tryin tuh hole me back! But it ain' dough. I get true, tuh de uderside. An pun de uderside my ashy foot step out pun de most beautiful grass. I never see a green so. I was so taken wit de grass I ain' even see de White girl come out dis big wall house. She come strait up tuh me an say, "you get catch by de Red Woman!" Den de girl jus laugh an point at de blood runnin down my leg. I get true but I still get catch. An even dough I run tuh Mr. Buyer shop fuh de salts faster dan de devil heself when I come home, we mummy dead.

LIBYA

> *(to WINSTON-JAMES)* I is acussin tuh Gracie talking a big
> bundle a foolishness, suh I kep kneadin de bread.
> I knead dat bread fuh so long, by de time I finish, it hard
> as cast iron.
> I shoulda t'row DAT at you muder,
> I woulda hit she too… right between de eyes.
> She was a bigger an slower target by dis time.
> Dat woulda close up she mout in trut.
> Den I coulda tek up my cast iron an dash out.
> If I'd a do dat, t'ings wouldn'ta end up so.

GRACIE

> *(quietly to LIBYA)* Libya der is still time tuh get me de
> salts. Doan wait till de last. *(wait)* Sittin in dis house is
> give me de belly. I ain' like you. I ain' know how you able
> tuh stan up in dis house wit gra'ma cryin out, RED
> WOMAN RED WOMAN alla dem years.
> I rader name de cane,
> An risk gettin catch again.
> But I ain' able wit dat now,
> Suh please Libya get me some salts.
> You lucky yuh ain' yet know dis pain.
> An still able tuh go out an name cane…
> I was fine when I was playin my namin game…

Scene 21

> *Inside Winston Sugar Cane Plantation.*
> *LIBYA age 20.*
> *GRACIE age 23.*
> *LIBYA leads GRACIE out into the cane field.*

LIBYA

> *(to WINSTON-JAMES)* I tell she strait, *(to GRACIE) I ain'*
> *gettin you salts, suh if yuh doan want my food let we go run*
> *dis cuttin out in de cane.*

GRACIE

> *(to LIBYA)* NO! No Libya yuh can' tek me out der, not in
> my condition… You guh long. I will wait fuh you inside.

Just get me some salts. I ain' care what kind you get. Anyt'ing will do… Epsom… table… kosher—

LIBYA

(to WINSTON-JAMES) I tek you muder out of de house fuh de first time in mumfs. I tell she strait, *We is gonna play a game. It's called name every piece a sugar cane in Winston Plantation… my plantation. Okay, I am gonna go dis way an you will go… dat way. Go!*

> *LIBYA turns away from GRACIE and starts naming cane.*

Okay, dem two der is Tracy an Clotell,
So close un'neat each uder,
T'inkin dem is as bless as we Lawrd Jesus' muder.
Oh lawrd, look Stacy Mae wit she eyes open up wide,
Holing pun she cast iron dat stuck tuh she side.
Now you mussy be Santiford der stannin up strait,
Spendin money at de track like it on a beautiful date.
Dis one must be name Margaret
Cause she face I cannot get
An you is look like Gracie
Eatin biscuit at high tea.
Oh look… dat one der is James. (LIBYA pretends to be GRACIE) *James… James!* (to GRACIE) *Wait where de blast is James?*

GRACIE

(GRACIE cries out.) James is gone. He gone Libya. He put dis cuttin in me an gone… an I need it tuh get out. Yuh gine help me or what? I just need some salts girl. Oh LAWRD I gine get catch in trut. Tek my han Libya. If you ain' gine give me salts at least tek my han. *(GRACIE gets hit with a sharp cutting pain.)* OH LAWRD—

LIBYA

(to GRACIE) I look at you muder outstretch han, an fuh de firs time I tell she dat, *I hope de Red Woman cut off you pig ears an rip out you loud mout… tear off you Black face an cuff you in you big teef!*

LIBYA turns to leave but stops in her tracks as the cane begins to rustle and she feels the Red Woman's approach.

Oh Lawrd! It gonna rain! IT GONNA RAIN! It gonna— *(She gets a cutting in her belly and speaks right to the Red Woman.)* You t'ink you gine catch me, but you can'. Just wait… just you wait nuh. I gine tek muh cast iron an mash up you face bad man!

GRACIE

(to LIBYA) Look Libya it ain' gonna rain. Come an tek my han, fuget de salts an just tek my han. We be fine if you just—
(GRACIE lifts her skirt as blood runs down her legs.) OH LAWRD it comin… it comin… De lawrd is fugiveness soul. You remember I tell you we mummy say everyt'ing is need a name or else it get tek up by de devil an die in shame. Cause I is gine have James Blackwell baby an we was gine name it—

GRACIE is hit with another cutting pain.

OH LAWRD!

Scene 22

Half in LIBYA's room, half in Winston Sugar Cane Plantation.
LIBYA age 75/20.
GRACIE age 23.

LIBYA

(to WINSTON-JAMES) Even dough she look me strait in de eye an I see de fright. Same fright in my gra'muder eye before she die… I still ain' give she my han… I just watch she. I watch she squeeze open she t'ick t'ighs, an fett wif she breaf heavy, holing pun de cane tuh kep she up till YOU fall from she belly. Wit she last bit a life you muder deliver you an den put yuh right intuh my arms. You was de first t'ing she ever give me.

GRACIE

(to LIBYA) Fugiveness is de way a de lawrd soul.
(GRACIE dies.)

LIBYA

(LIBYA looks down at the baby, WINSTON-JAMES and
speaks to him as the cutting pain in her belly continues to
build.) You fall like brea'fruit does fall from de tree,
When everyt'ing is calm.
No man choppin at it trunk.
No wind shakin it's leaves.
My gra'muder blame de boys who is climb de tree fuh de
fallen brea'fruit but I know de boys is not to blame.
It is de tree who tell de branch tuh let go.

LIBYA picks up WINSTON-JAMES.

I was de only one lef suh I had tuh name you cause
everyt'ing is need a name or else it get tek up by de devil
an die in shame. I mean, I ain' even know if it was too
late cause by de time Gracie put you intuh my arms you
was... you was already gone... you was—
Suh I berry you.
I mean maybe I shoulda tek she han, cause den... den
maybe... you or you muder might have—
But I ain'... I just berry you. (LIBYA begins to bury
WINSTON-JAMES in the cane field.)
But, but I—I, I name you, I name you Winston-James
Blackwell cause you had you muder big mout an an you
fader Black skin. So Black I ca hardly see you. Except fuh
you big eyes— (The cutting pain in LIBYA's belly is so
intense she stops digging, silence.)
(LIBYA begins to confesses to the Red Woman, to WINSTON-
JAMES, to herself.) Oh lawrd... I lef...
I was suh scared I lef. I lef you an you muder in de cane.
I even lef my gra'muder cast iron in she house even
dough I could have it now. I just lef an I kep on leffin till
I eventually lef an come alla de way here. I been here fuh
over forty years. I ain' t'ink de Red Woman gine come alla
de way up here... but she do cause I still here wit my

belly startin tuh cut an no where tuh run.
Suh what I escape?

> *LIBYA looks at her hands and then cries for the first
> and last time, her pain begins to subside she speaks
> partly to the Red Woman and partly to the WINSTON-
> JAMES she created in her mind.*

I would like fuh you tuh take my han…
It will do, even dough what I really want is food… mek
up in my cast iron dat as black as… What I really want is
some food tuh tek me true. Just a small amount would
do. At dis age I ain' able tuh get my colen blown out my
ass wit gas. But fuhget dat, it too late fuh dat, muh cast
iron ain' here an visitin hours long over. An I ain' want
nuh nurse comin in here… checkin un'neat my bed fuh
visitor… telling me it sound like I holing a party up in
here. I rader she stan where she is, smokin she guts out
by de back a de buildin. Suh come, tek my hand an let we
go. *(LIBYA waits with her hand outstretched.)*

> *Lights fade to black.*
> *The end.*